Straight fr

Hea. ᵕ

First published in 1999 by

Wilbek & Lewbar
90 Victoria Road, Devizes
Wiltshire, SN10 1EU

Author Nicholas Winn
Editor Bob Wilson
Illustrations Tamsin Cook
Design & Layout Emma Wilson

Printed in Great Britain

ISBN 1 901284 19 0

Dedication

This book is dedicated to my mother,
brothers and Sheila

Introduction

Nicholas Winn was born in Bristol, the eldest of three boys. His mother Joyce is a Londoner, now living in Bristol and, was married to Harry a Yorkshireman who sadly died in 1981.

Nicholas has been a nurse now for some thirty years and is currently working part-time as a nurse at a local nursing home. He lives with his partner Sheila, her son and mother. They reside in a large comfy family house in Midsomer Norton.

An avid nature lover, he is often seen out cycling in the local countryside, gaining inspiration and maintaining some degree of fitness! He also enjoys painting with water colours, reading and the occasional visit to the theatre or cinema. When time permits, he enjoys swimming, weight training and yoga. Also, participating in the martial art of 'Taekwondo'.

Nicholas feels that poetry isn't given the recognition it deserves and is committed to doing something about it. He says *"Poetry is one of the finest tools for self expression!"*

Contents

Our Alice

Our Alice kept the corner shop, since just before the war,
It's still the same as way back then, in nineteen thirty four.
She's run it as a Post Office and kept it all intact,
But now they want to change things and, to have our Alice sacked.

She knows the local children and she loves to give them treats,
Like chews and sticks of liquorice, and inexpensive sweets.
Old people like to go there, just to draw their pensions out,
Or visit for a chat to hear, the gossip that's about.

She's a mine of information, like the 'Citizen's Advice',
If you've got an awkward question, she can answer in a trice.
She may not have the answer, but you don't get sent away,
Our Alice will investigate and ring you back that day.

She's kept her records tidily, is accurate and true,
Can keep a level head and smile, whenever there's a queue.
Our Alice is so businesslike, efficient, shrewd and quick,
She's sprightly and a stalwart, and has never been off sick.

What right's this thing called progress, got to hassle and dictate,
And send our lovely Alice to, an ignominious fate?
Full marks to her for closing and for never giving in,
To the whims of a computer, and its electronic din.

Good luck to you our Alice, from the people you once served,
At last you've found the dignity, you have so long deserved.

By N Winn

Green fingers

I remember in my childhood, how I loved to plant a twig,
No longer than a ruler, just a cutting or a sprig.
Thrust down into the earth it was, no effort did I make,
Surprisingly it didn't die, but always seemed to take.

I'd water it religiously, and must have cast a spell,
Because of how it sprouted and, seemed to do so well.
I must have planted dozens, and it swelled my sense of pride,
To watch them grow in spring, and know not one of them had died.

My roses always flowered and the buddleia would shoot,
I don't know how I did it but, the privet grew a root.
I grew so much forsythia, I gave a lot away,
And wouldn't be surprised, if some were flourishing today.

I'm thankful for the garden and my little plot of ground,
And the gift which I inherited, that mightn't have been found.
For in my happy childhood, how could I have foreseen,
I'd always love the garden, and my fingers would be green!

by N Winn

Sunrise over Somerset

It's sunrise over Somerset and rooks rise with a caw,
As early morning sun burns red, on Glastonbury Tor.
A sea of mist encircles it, as night's cool breath exhales,
Through ebbing tides of darkness, fast retreating over Wales.

A silence soaks the stillness, which has yet to fade away,
Like frost which melts in meadows, in the sun's first warming ray.
Though the pace of day's momentum, starts to stir the earth from sleep,
Long lie the ghosts of Somerset, in slumber soft and deep.

When the skies turn blue to brighten with the door of day ajar,
And you gaze beyond the Quantocks and the Mendip Hills afar.
You can hear the cattle breathing, as they chew the Sedgemoor cud,
And the shrieking of the seagulls, in the distant Weston mud.

Do you sense the rising sun begins to cheer you, as you start,
To realise that Somerset, can captivate your heart.
Especially when you can see the morning has been kissed,
With a golden touch of sunlight, on the essence of the mist.

By N Winn

Television gripes

You sit there gawking at my screen, and films I'm forced to show,
Content you've got the power, that can make me stop or go.
You change my channels madly, in a manner underhand,
With a tatty bit of plastic, which you play with in your hand.

Why do I have to stand here, as the empty hours pass,
In fear of when your duster, stirs the static on my glass?
You rub your eyes too often, when you should be up in bed,
But you'd rather sprawl in front of me and stare at me instead.

I'm never temperamental and I rarely go on strike,
God help me if I do because you do just what you like.
You thump me on my casing, give my cathode tube a shake,
Then belt me round the plug holes, causing terminals to break.

You've tipped a pint of beer on me and made me blow a fuse,
Subjected me to videos and torrents of abuse.
Your cat climbs on my table and annoys me with its purr,
Then hassles me with fleas and blocks my aerial with fur.

You've thrown your slippers at me, if you've not liked what you see,
But little do you realise, I'm only a TV.
Your flesh and blood created me and sold me from a shop,
So idiots like you can sit and watch, my screen non stop!

By N Winn

The arthritic haunted house

Have you noticed in the house sometimes at night, when you're alone,
It makes those eerie noises, which can chill you to the bone.
In ours you'll hear a clomping sound, like burglars on the stairs,
Or squeaking from the lounge, as if they're bouncing on the chairs.

For many years I used to hear a hissing in the hall,
Which sounded like a snake was trying, to slither down the wall.
I'd fear it was a python, or a cobra from the zoo,
And not my human neighbour, everytime he flushed the loo.

Although the house is ancient and arthritic to the core,
Because of all its creakings and the groanings from the floor,
I've never known arthritis pound, like footsteps in the night,
Or whisper in the bedroom, when there's nobody in sight.

The house is plumbed with miles of pipes, which swish around and bump,
Each one of them's connected, to the bathroom and a pump.
Now in a house like this, that's unpredictable and weird,
All thumps of pumps and bumping should, be analysed or feared!

I'd swear the cellar's haunted, though the spirits seem aloof,
Just like the agile ghosts which kick, the moss down off the roof.
It could be them that cause the doors to open and to shut,
Or make the wretched light bulbs ping and go out with a 'phut!'

If you think your house is scary and arthritic, do be kind,
It could be dark and haunted like, the nightmare which is mine!

By N Winn

Old Fred the milkman

For sixty years he's pounded rounds, in wind and rain and cold,
He does them just the same today, at eighty two years old.
When you hear the chink of pinta's and a whistle at the gate,
You'll know old Fred's delivering, because he's never late.

With his cheery disposition and an old and battered coat,
He'll brighten winter mornings, with his bottles and his float.
If you stop and have a chat with him, he'll open up his heart,
And tell you how he did his rounds, with just a horse and cart.

He's a pillar of society, a proud and loyal man,
Who's always so obliging that, he'll help you when he can.
If you're going on a holiday, just leave the key with Fred,
He'll check the house to keep it safe and see the fish are fed.

If you want old fashioned service, then on Fred you can depend,
He's kindly and good natured, and to the old a friend.
If a customer's in trouble, or they need an errand run,
Old Fred'll find a bit of time, to see a favour's done.

There's talk of him retiring and if the rumour's true,
He'll have had a worthy innings, at the age of eighty two.
Although he's irreplaceable, there cannot be complaint,
And I'm sure that when he dies, he'll be remembered as a saint!

By N Winn

The thirty plastic bags of a bag lady

I'm just a humble bag lady, content to walk and roam,
This maze of city streets, which are my rather messy home.
I've always been a simple sort, who lives in dirty rags,
Whose only worldly goods, are shoved in thirty plastic bags!

Don't ask me why there's thirty, it's quite possible there's more,
I've kept them since I hit the streets, in nineteen fifty four.
I had a dodgy marriage and my husband was a lout,
But it had a happy ending, 'cos I left him and walked out!

It can be quite a lonely life, but characters you meet,
Will sometimes slip you coppers, and a bit of lunch to eat.
I'll sleep in cold shop doorways, just depending how I feel,
Or down the 'Sally Army', if I'm dying for a meal!

I guess I'm pretty hardy, and I'm used to being cold,
But I do begin to wonder, what'll happen when I'm old?
It's often very tiring, carting thirty bags about,
Especially with my bunions and the God forsaken gout!

I know you're keen to see what's in the bags, but I suppose,
You've got a right to know and I should say it's mostly clothes.
This red one is my special one, for toiletries and shoes,
And this is just my make up bag, for use in public loos!

The weather never bothers me, the rain and things like that,
I simply use a plastic bag, which makes a lovely hat.
If it's sunny in the summer, then the park's a super place,
To lie out in the sunshine, with a bag across your face!

I know I'm not immortal, and my time is bound to come,
But when I die, my plastic bags must number thirty one!
I want to be cremated, and my ashes they must save,
Sealed in a plastic bag, with all the others in my grave!

by N Winn

My lovely prickly cactus

I used to keep a desert, in my bedroom in a pot,
A miniature Sahara, though the room was seldom hot!
There were palm trees made of plastic, an oasis made of tin,
With a funny little hole through which, you poured the water in.

The focal point was something, that was over eight foot tall,
A huge Opuntia cactus, with a name I can't recall.
It towered in a corner, like a green enormous thumb,
Which left my mother daunted, and my father overcome.

I must say it was beautiful, in spite of all its spines,
A masterpiece in succulent, or spiky plant designs!
I never saw it flower, and it never bore a fruit,
But it made me really happy, 'cos I thought its shape was cute.

I hardly ever watered it, or fed it with manure,
Just poked the soil around it, with the handle of a skewer.
I used to sit and chat to it, or moan if I was low,
I'm sure this was a stimulus and prompted it to grow:

One night I heard a crashing and a scattering of sand,
Which jolted me from dreaming, like a liner striking land.
I fumbled for the light switch and in its brilliance saw,
My lovely prickly cactus, had collapsed onto the floor!

I'll never know what caused it, and such things are hard to gauge,
But I think it was the pampering, good living, and old age!!

By N Winn

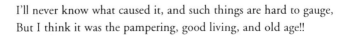

Spidery thoughts in the bath

I creep up through the plumbing, when the humans are asleep,
Past hairs and bits of toenail, where the water lingers deep.
A tube of plastic piping, is to me an easy path,
To crawl up and investigate, if someone's in the bath.

I hope and pray there isn't, for the bath is my domain,
For courting round the 'U' bend, and high diving down the drain.
I'll slalom round the plug hole for a laugh, and then perhaps,
Attempt to scale the steepest bit, to fiddle with the taps.

I haven't made it yet! but if that hallowed day should come,
I'll be the only blighter that's, climbed higher than the scum.
I've tried so many times, although I must be rather smug,
Because I end up falling off, and landing on the plug.

I hate it when the bath is wet and slime is on my slope,
Or if when I'm out prowling , I should step in lumps of soap.
I'd rather surf the lavatory, the bidet or endure,
A holiday in darkness, in the cellar or the sewer.

In case you start to wonder, what this rhyme is all about,
I'm big and black and hairy, and there isn't that much doubt,
You treat me like an enemy, when really I'm a friend,
For I'm the great big spider, that you washed around the bend!!!

By N Winn

The dusty dinner plate

On a rainy day last winter, when I cleaned a cupboard out,
I came upon a plate, which raised an element of doubt.
A doubt about its usefulness, or place of origin,
Though one thing seemed quite certain, that its place was in the bin.

It sparkled through its dustiness, as if to say to me,
"Don't throw me out because of doubt, be careful don't you see,
I'm worth more than the rubbish tip, look closer, take a peek,
I'm not a dusty dinner plate, but priceless and antique!"

I'd watched the 'Antique's Roadshow', not too many days before,
The plate was rather beautiful, so how could I be sure?
I brushed away its dustiness, to see what was revealed,
And had to think its loveliness, at once to me appealed.

I took it to a friend, who knew a bit about old plates,
He said it was a something but, he couldn't find the dates.
I let him take it with him and that left me reassured,
Next day he phoned me up to say, "I hope your plate's insured!"

He really was ecstatic, and the truth was soon unfurled,
He said 'It's worth a million, it's the rarest in the world!'
From then I knew just what to do, an option I must make,
Decide to keep or sell it, and to see it doesn't break.
It wasn't long before I thought 'This really isn't fair,
What good's to me a plate when, I can be a millionaire!'

By N Winn

My old trusty spirited alarm clock

A clock I owned in childhood, was as solid as a rock,
It had a trusty spirit and could take an awful knock.
For nearly every morning, when I cancelled the alarm,
I'd knock it off the table, yet it never came to harm.

I think it was my grannies, but I never was quite sure,
My mother said she'd bought it, up in London in the war.
She told me it was mass produced and hence, the price was cheap,
I bet she never thought its tick ,would lull me off to sleep.

It stood so proudly by my bed, right underneath the light,
Its hands were green and luminous, and glowed like eyes at night.
Sometimes it needed cleaning and would end up in disgrace,
Because it always stopped, unless I put it on its face!

It had around its battered glass, a lovely metal rim,
Which I could shine and polish, just to keep it looking trim.
The figures were old fashioned, and its little hand was bent,
But the clock was always accurate, and thankfully it went.

In the psychedelic sixties, when bright colours were the scene,
I oiled the clock and painted it, a phosphorescent green.
I don't think it enjoyed this and it stuck forevermore,
With paint around its mainspring, at exactly half past four!

By N Winn

17

Hoarding problems

I know there's ten commandments, but I think there ought to be,
Another that's appropriate, for characters like me.
A law that's passed by Government, to leave me in no doubt,
That hoarding's not illegal, if I'm loath to throw things out.

My wardrobe's an example, of the thing I'm trying to say,
It's full of ancient clothing, that I ought to throw away.
A kaftan from the sixties, and a Beatles suit that's neat,
And fifty pairs of socks I know, will never meet my feet.

The cupboard's full to bursting, with a hundred pairs of pants,
Not one of them's attractive, or conducive to romance.
They share the drawers with hankies, that have never blown a nose,
And dozens of old cardigans, I think my mother chose.

It isn't only clothing, that for rainy days I keep,
It's the bills, receipts and paperwork, at least a metre deep.
Old after shave and Christmas gifts, like powder and shampoo,
And all the other useless things, that disinfect the loo!

If you think my bathroom's cluttered, then the kitchen's even worse.
The lack of room to store things, is becoming quite a curse.
I've hoarded pans and saucepans, plastic bags and piles of plates,
And tins of food and rusty cans, long past their sell by dates.

The garden must be mentioned and it's now I take the chance,
To say it's like a jungle, 'cos I've hoarded all the plants.
The garage is a rubbish tip, I don't know where things are,
One day I'll chuck it out perhaps, and maybe find the car.

Until it's time for me to die, I'll hoard for all I'm worth,
Then when I get to Heaven, I'll continue like on Earth!

By N Winn

A visit to the newsagent

A visit to the newsagent, is not the stuff of dreams,
Especially when you need to read, the monthly magazines.
The ones with massive muscle men, or other glossy mags,
All looking very tempting, but concealed in plastic bags!
Or if you want to buy a card, whatever that may be,
It takes you twenty minutes, just to find the code or key.
You think the one you've chosen's, inexpensive and OK,
Until you're charged a fiver, when you take it down to pay.
It can be so relaxing, when the hand of time allows,
To stroll among the novels and the stationery to browse.
It's best when staff are busy, and they have no time to look,
You can stay and read a chapter, from the months best selling book.
And not to mention newspapers, the mainstay of the shop,
Without them all the custom and the profiting would stop!
They're always so accessible, to grateful eyes like this,
Who want to read the headlines and to give the rest a miss!
A visit to the newsagent, could bring you fame and wealth,
Or problems with the pocket, and eventually your health!
You could flutter on the lottery, strike lucky with the bets,
Or spend your money lavishly, on sweets and cigarettes.

By N Winn

A quaint old fashioned bookshop

There's nothing like old bookshops and spending hours lost,
In brown and fusty pages, when there isn't any cost.
No price incurred for standing, or for sitting down to browse,
In funny old surroundings, for as long as time allows.

Just leafing through the paperbacks, and novels stained by age,
Brings pleasure to some people, that's impossible to gauge.
Myself, I like a nature book, the classics or a play,
Or fat encyclopaedias, to while an hour away.

I'll often find a bargain, that I'd love to read in bed,
That's only held together, by a staple or a thread.
Although there's missing pages, and it's almost torn in two,
A little bit of sellotape, will leave the book as new.

Not only do I like the books, the atmosphere and smells,
I really love the magazines, that clutter up the shelves.
Who cares about the dustiness, or dog ears and the grime,
A quaint old fashioned bookshop's, just the place for passing time!

By N Winn

Words of advice to all aspiring poets

These poems that you're reading and attempting to recite,
Are anything but easy, or just leisurely to write.
You'll need a good vocabulary, a dictionary as well,
And it helps if you're a clever bod, who learnt at school to spell.

Although it's fairly difficult ,there's no need to rehearse,
You put your pen to paper and, just hope it writes a verse.
If you wait for inspiration, then you'll waste a lot of time,
Just string some words together and, attempt to make them rhyme.

Try writing to a rhythm, but don't beat it on a drum,
It helps to count the syllables, a clever rule of thumb.
Don't ever use a long word, when a shorter one will do,
Or write too many verses, keep it down to forty two.

If you want to be a poet then, you ought to pick your nose,
It helps the concentration, and will see the metre flows.
Keep studying your 'Wordsworth' and 'Hardy', and your 'Hood',
One day you'll write a poem and it might be really good!

By N Winn

Extractor fans

Extractor fans are whirring, with impatience on a wall,
Beyond a barbed wire fence, which looks barbaric, cruel and tall.
An alien stink is wafting, through a copse of jagged trees,
Malingering in a fog, which makes the nose and senses sneeze.

Extractor fans are moaning, like a monster fresh from hell,
Expelling something awful, with a nasty toxic smell.
Convulvulus and brambles, and a vast amount of rust,
Are crumbling on the pathway, in a cloud of poison dust.

Extractor fans are hissing, like a snake about to bite,
All spitting out their venom, at the silence of the night.
A tongue of flame is searing, up a chimney to the sky,
Is this the lethal reason, why a forest had to die?

Extractor fans are whizzing, with an urgency to clear,
A monstrous chest of toxins, which the villagers all fear.
They fought to try and stop it, but the planners went ahead,
No wonder all the flowers and the foliage are dead.

By N Winn

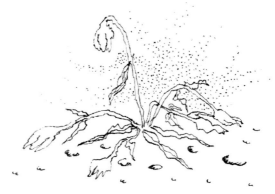

The heart

(In Praise Of Somerset Coal Mines)

On tranquil fields of Somerset, the coal dust used to lie,
Beneath the pit head wheel stood tall, rotating through the sky.
I watch it now beyond the elms, surreal between the heaps,
Still turning with a passion where, the ghost of mining sleeps.

I hear the happy clamour of old miners, cheeks aglow,
As east winds numb a morning, round black slag heaps in the snow.
They're moaning at the prospect, of a sadness up ahead,
When the coal is sealed forever in, the Earth's eternal bed.

I see its chimney smoking now, and smoke begin to lift,
To smudge the ashen sky before, the early morning shift.
The shaft begins to echo, with the voices of brave men,
About to face redundancy, who'll never work again.

The wind is in the wires and it's whispering a tune,
Of how a heart is dying and how death will still it soon.
But the heart beats deep in Somerset, through methane and the oil,
And its spirit pounds forever, in the silence of the soil.

By N Winn

George

(The source of those mysteries which occur around the house)

George comes to visit often, though invisible he is,
I'm certain he's responsible, for life's great mysteries.
Like when you know you've had something, but find it rather weird,
Because it's gone for walkies and, completely disappeared.

He popped in fairly recently, with supernatural power,
To pinch a bunch of keys from me, at some ungodly hour.
His actions are unwelcome and, can cause unpleasant shocks,
Especially when you're keyless, and you have to change the locks.

One time he came to see me, in the middle of the night,
When once again his actions, gave me problems and a fright.
He can't have liked the mirror, that was hanging in the hall,
For when I woke next morning, it had fallen off the wall.

He's very unpredictable and seems to like to climb,
So well can I remember, the most catastrophic time.
When George shinned up the chimney, with a bomb tied to his foot,
And left the wretched living room, six inches deep in soot.

Things happen in the house sometimes, which leave the patience strained,
Because they're inconveniencing, and often unexplained.
Don't feel too much resentment though, a friendship's there to forge,
Just leave a bit of supper, and a fiver out for George!

By N Winn

Old Albert

Old Albert goes out every day, no matter what it's like,
More often he'll be walking, but he's sometimes on his bike.
He'll always wear the overcoat, he bought when times were poor,
And a hat which was the fashion, in the years before the war.

His shoes are brave survivors, from the days when shoes were made,
To last through active service, and cold mornings on parade.
His trusty stick is with him, but he doesn't need support,
Because he's strong and sturdy, rather resolute and short.

If a lady passes in the street, he'll stop and doff his hat,
Be keen to bid good morning and get ready for a chat.
His face is round and rosy, and his words are warm and wise,
The smile is always wide, because there's gladness in his eyes.

His hobby is his garden, which he loves to dig and tend,
And although he is a widower, he has a lady friend.
Though Albert's in his eighties, he's a man to take a chance,
By betting on the horses, or just going to a dance.

A local man and proud of it, he built his house alone,
With vast amount of patience, and two lorry loads of stone!
He'll turn his hand to anything, and do it by himself,
Because he's independent, and won't ask for any help.

Old Albert's generation, are alas a dying breed,
Born in the simple days, before technology and speed.
I hope that when he dies, and meets his Maker's peace and grace,
There'll be another gentleman, to take Old Albert's place!

By N Winn

I think I've found the happiness

In the brightness of a May day, with its blossom scented air,
Hum insects in the hedgerows, and the meadows everywhere.
With the ravages of winter past, soon summer nights will heal,
The memories of gales and frosts, as cold as tempered steel.

A kiss of sunlight bursts the buds, the pulse of life now quakes,
It throbs down in the forest, as all dormant life awakes.
The swallows must have sensed it ,as they're starting to arrive,
And the bees are looking busy, as they buzz around their hive.

The leaves are growing greener, as the blossom petals fall,
And sunlight strengthens daily, in its splendour over all.
Sweet music of the blackbird, adds some essence to the hush,
Swelled later by the flutings, of the robin and a thrush.

The loveliness of flowers, in the garden now excels,
At titillating senses, with their colours and their smells.
The gardener is busy, with his vegetables and seeds,
And I think I've found the happiness, the human spirit needs.

By N Winn

The leonids

Last night I woke at three o clock and gazed out at the skies,
Which yawned into the universe and down onto my eyes.
Ten thousand stars like distant ships, blazed far away in space,
As a crescent moon slouched in the east, ashamed to show her face.

Faint was its moonlight on the path, and frost had taken hold,
To turn to steel the frozen earth, and lock it up with cold.
A stream of silence floated through, the lake of night so deep,
You could almost sense the living world, was calm and fast asleep.

No breath or breeze exhaled, into the stillness of the hour,
No movement stirred the starlight, or the magic of its power.
Just rhythms of life's essence, kept on humming out their tune,
As I stared in contemplation, at the softness of the moon.

The stage seemed set for something, then I saw a streak of light,
Another and another, till the heavens were alight.
And then it was I realised, just as the experts said,
Tonight's the night the 'Leonids', would sparkle overhead!

By N Winn

*Leonids- A shower of
meteors, seen recently
in the late night skies.*

A home

A home is only pleasing, if it's full of pleasant things,
Which bolster life's enjoyment and the happiness this brings.
It needs a cosy living room, where cares of day decrease,
Because there is a welcome, in an ambience of peace.

The kitchen should be brimming, with an oil of love and filled,
With life's most tender graces, which are warm and never chilled.
Their essence must be near to hand, for all who unawares,
Might want to wander through to reach, the hallway and the stairs.

The bathroom and the bedroom's where serenity should be,
Where rest and relaxation come with ease, and always see,
That warmth and comfort radiate, and glow within the walls,
To cheer the hearts of visitors and anyone who calls.

It isn't wealth and furniture, or ornaments alone,
That make the happy atmosphere, so vital to a home.
A home is only homely, if between its roof and floor,
Are feeling's that are tranquil and will last forevermore.

By N Winn

Spirit in my stride

(on frosty early morning walks)

On those misty frosty mornings, when the rime was on the grass,
And the earth was hard like iron, and the pond had turned to glass.
When the moon was sharp and sinking, from the fast retreating night,
I loved to go out walking, with the winter at its height.

To wrap up was a pleasure and to start off with a stroll,
Would energise my heart and then, revitalise my soul.
I'd step the pace up slowly, through an ice encrusted lane,
And crunch through frozen puddles, that had lingered after rain.

I well remember cawing of the rooks, in naked trees,
The crispy white appearance, of the hedgerows and the leas.
How wonderful the moment, with the sun about to rise,
When the essence of the night would turn, to fire in the skies.

I still recall the numbness in my fingers, then the sting,
As blood would start to circulate, and warm them up to bring,
A sense of great enlightenment and energy inside,
Which helped to lift me up, and put some spirit in my stride.

By N Winn

The cellar

The cellar used to creak beneath the floorboards in our house,
My father used to say, it was a monster or a mouse!
At dead of night I'm sure, I heard a creature crawling round,
But when we looked next morning, there was nothing to be found.

The cellar door was rotten and would open with a groan,
I wouldn't dare to open it, if I was on my own!
I know there was a ghostly shape, that reared up by the door,
It looked a bit like 'Satan', but I couldn't tell for sure.

One day my father took me down, to try and ease my mind,
I couldn't hardly speak because, of fears of what I'd find!
There were lots of spooky cupboards, like old coffins in disguise,
And cobwebs full of spiders, with enormous beady eyes.

The walls had cracks between them, where a dinosaur could hide,
Or nasty little demons, which were mad and evil eyed!
It smelt just like a cellar should, a dungeon or a cave,
And I'm sure down on the floor there were, the remnants of a grave.

One night I was awakened, by an eerie scratching sound,
Which gave way to a moaning, that had caused my heart to pound!
I crept in to my father, to tell him what I'd heard,
At first he said I'd dreamt it, but then, he said 'Absurd!'
We tiptoed downstairs gingerly, it must have been a rat,
But when the door creaked open, out shot the angry cat!

By N Winn

The christmas rush

The Christmas rush has started and the cards are in the shops,
It makes me really wonder, if the rushing ever stops!
Sweet muzak canned as carols, is reverberating loud,
I bet if it was rock-and-roll, it wouldn't be allowed.

Old Santa's in his grotto, as the children queue with glee,
Three pounds a child, with discount if a mum has more than three!
There's holly round the checkout and a forest overhead,
Of Christmas decorations, in green and white and red.

The traffic queues are thickening, and so are all the fumes,
As Silent Night with anything, but silence loudly booms!
The plastic slap of credit cards, is added to the bills,
As Christmas greeting shopping bags, are bursting by the tills.

Bright Christmas lights are swinging, in the silence of the sky,
Adorning every tree or bush, that dares to greet the eye!
A million 'Merry Christmases' are tinkling out a tune,
Which seems to me peculiar, because it's only June!

By N Winn

The scales of life

The scales of life are shaky and it seems as if to me,
Too many people suffer, from the weight of misery.
If only we could lighten it to make the burden fair,
Replacing it with happiness, for everyone to share!

The scales of life are wobbly, which can only serve to mean,
That those who 'have' are happy, and the 'have not's' only dream.
Perhaps a bit of giving, by the 'haves' to those in need,
Will help restore equality, and stem the tide of greed!

The scales of life are straining, with the heaviness of hate,
Which needs to be removed, before they break and it's too late.
Too late to stop them spinning, to a fate forevermore,
Bogged down with instability, and growing threats of war!

The scales of life seem loaded, with a history of woe,
Of hunger, grief and poverty, which never seem to go.
How lovely if the future saw, their slant to sadness cease,
And evermore the sway of years, be influenced by peace!

By N Winn

High blood cholesterol!

When you've lived for half a century, you suffer aches and pains,
Which seem to get much worse, each time it's cold or when it rains.
Although you're hale and healthy, it's the time of life to see,
Your heart's in good condition and there's nothing in your wee!

You go down to the doctor's and he does his doctor's bit,
Then when he's finished prodding, he pronounces you as fit.
He finds you've got a blood pressure, that's just a bit too high,
But tries to reassure you, that you're not about to die.

He'll take a spot of blood, and with cholesterol in mind,
Advises you to wait and see, just what the 'vampires' find.
"Just telephone the surgery, about a week'll do!"
You wished you'd never rang, because it's up at six point two.

Your past life runs before you, as you ponder what went wrong,
'I've never been a smoker, I'm a runner and I'm strong.
I'm careful with my diet and I'm hardly overweight,
So just what's to become of me and what'll be my fate?"

Once more the doctor tells you, not to worry on his breath,
(Not really any comfort, when you're on the verge of death).
But then you change your attitude, your outlook and your stance,
By thinking life's an innings and, there's not another chance.

'To hell with all the experts and their erudite advice,
I'll do just what I want because, it's me who'll pay the price.
I'm going out to celebrate, this splendid bit of news,
By spending all my savings, on my partner and a cruise!"

By N Winn

Life's a fertile garden

Life's a fertile garden, we should till and cultivate,
To make it hard for weeds to grow, like misery and hate.
If we use the tools of gentleness and goodness every day,
We'll keep its essence beautiful and weeds of hate away.

If only spores of anger, could be sterilised to see,
There never was a chance for them, to reach maturity.
They'd leave a space for happiness and seeds of love to grow,
Which only caring hands could learn, to nurture and to sow.

The soil of time is mellowed, with emotion and our years,
Which seep into the past, to show in laughter and in tears.
If the future's to be fruitful, so the flowers of joy increase,
We must strive to be unselfish, and to live our lives in peace.

By N Winn

My patient colleague

How wonderfully the flame of love can sometimes start to flare,
Especially when you're lonely and you think nobody's there!
It's funny how its energy, can suddenly burn through,
Just as in my experience, with somebody I knew.

I'd worked with her for many years and never gave a thought,
She'd think of me as somebody, to love and maybe court!
She picked her moment wisely, and she took me by surprise,
Because she was determined and had purpose in her eyes.

I'd suffered a relationship that faltered and had died,
With someone who was insecure, and never satisfied!
I'd often seek solutions, from my colleagues and a friend,
Of what they thought I ought to do, to bring things to an end.

I had no cause to worry, and the answer came along,
Just as it always seems to do, when love and life are wrong!
She'd found another man and solved my problems at a glance,
And gave my colleague hope, that she was now in with a chance.

The chance to cheer me up and, give my loneliness a shove,
And seal its vacant space up, with her happiness and love!
Since then we've been together and have never been apart,
Because she knew just what to do, to captivate my heart!!!

By N Winn

Thoughts of an elderly lady
(about to be moved into a nursing home)

'They think I'm old and wandering, and can no longer cope,
So they've gone and found a bed for me, they think might offer hope.
It's in a lavish nursing home, not far away from here,
With a lovely en suite bathroom and, it isn't very dear:

They've told me all about it, and are quite content to pay,
To take my independence, and my cosy home away!
"You'll have your meals provided, and they'll help you dress and wash,
It really is a palace and, it's clean and rather posh"!

I've been a private person now, for sixty years or more,
The prospect of a nursing home, is dreadful and I'm sure,
I'll die before six months is up, because I really hate,
The thought of being toiletted, and being made to wait!

'We'll take you down on Sunday, just to let you have a look,
Imagine no more housework, and you'll never have to cook.
Your meals will be provided, no more shopping trips or chores!'
Quite honestly I think my life's, about to lose its cause.

I might be slightly muddled, not as sprightly as I was,
But I've always been hard working and have managed well because,
I'd hate to be a burden on my daughter and her spouse,
Who want to take my liberty, and sell my lovely house!

By N Winn

Illustrated Poetry Books

Other Poetry Titles in the series:

Dreams of the Raven	ISBN 1 901284 01 8	£3.00 inc p&p
The Spirit of Christmas	ISBN 1 901284 08 5	£3.50 inc p&p
Circles of Love	ISBN 1 901284 03 4	£3.50 inc p&p
Memories of a Wiltshire Farmer	ISBN 1 901284 04 2	£3.50 inc p&p
Memories of a Wilts Farmer Wife	ISBN 1 901284 15 8	£3.85 inc p&p
Meditating Dreams	ISBN 1 901284 07 7	£3.75 inc p&p
This Wonderful World	ISBN 1 901284 06 9	£3.75 inc p&p
Life's a Laugh	ISBN 1 901284 09 3	£3.75 inc p&p
Life's Little Miracles	ISBN 1 901284 10 7	£3.75 inc p&p
Earth's Rhapsody	ISBN 1 901284 11 5	£3.85 inc p&p
Candlelight Visions	ISBN 1 901284 14 X	£3.95 inc p&p
Memories from the Attic	ISBN 1 901284 13 1	£3.95 inc p&p
Spirit of a Loving Heart	ISBN 1 901284 16 6	£3.95 inc p&p
Whispers in the Garden of Dreams	ISBN 1 901284 17 4	£3.95 inc p&p
Wings of the Brave (RAF)	ISBN 1 901284 12 3	£4.00 inc p&p
Bombers' Moon (RAF)	ISBN 1 901284 18 2	£4.25 inc p&p

If you would like to know more about our illustrated poetry books or order any of the above titles (Cheques payable to Wilbek & Lewbar), then do contact us at:

Wilbek & Lewbar
90 Victoria Road, Devizes, Wiltshire, SN10 1EU, England
Tel / Fax: 01380 720271   E-mail: wil.bar@zetnet.co.uk